Central Italy: The Mar(

Enrico Massetti

Central Italy: The Marches and Abruzzo
Enrico Massetti
Copyright Enrico Massetti 2015
Published by Enrico Massetti
All Rights Reserved
ISBN: 978-1-329-71535-6

From Pesaro to Roccaraso

The Marches and the Abruzzi are a part of Italy not very well known to the international tourist. It is not just a question of doing justice to these areas by recommending them to the tourist; the tourist himself will make some fascinating discoveries, because these areas are no less rich in art treasures and natural beauties than others much more famous.

There are mighty Roman ruins, wonderful churches and abbeys, Renaissance palaces, picture galleries rich, particularly in works of the Venetian School (to know the rare works of Crivelli or Lotto, one must visit the galleries of the Marches).

Then there is the majestic mountain scenery of the Maiella and the Gran Sasso, and the long golden sands of the Adriatic beaches.

There is yet another reason for visiting these parts. Everyone. knows of the exploits of the other peoples of Italy, the Eruscans in the north and the Greeks in the south: but these peoples, even if they became acclimatized, were foreigners, they came from beyond the sea. The Marches and Umbria were populated and civilized by native people, the Italic. On this route, we shall pass through the ruins of an ancient city, Corfinium.

In 90 BC the people of this city rose against Rome, and made it the capital of their state, giving it a name destined to have a very long life – Italia. That ancient Italia was overwhelmed and defeated. But the name remained, and long outlived Roman power, to spread to the whole of Italy.

Pesaro

Pesaro still has fine monuments dating from the time when it was a Signory, first of the Malatesta, and then of the Sforza and the Della Revere: the Ducal Palace (15th cent.) and the Costanza Fortress by Laurana. From here, passing the Romanesque Cathedral we arrive at Palazzo Toschi-Mosca, with the most important Majolica Museum in Italy, and the rich Picture Gallery (great Coronation of the Virgin by Giovanni Bellini, works by Michele di Malice, Beccafumi etc.). From here we can go on to Sant'Agostino with its magnificent Gothic portal of 1413.

About 2 km. (1 1/4 mi.) out of the city, on a height near the sea, is Villa Imperiale (15th – 16th cent.) of which the Emperor Frederick III laid the foundation stone, a luxurious noble dwelling of the 15th century, with noteworthy frescoes by Dossi, Bronzino, Perin del Vaga.

Pesaro-Urbino district is wetting by the Adriatic sea: it is known for its "maioliche", the parks, the castles and its artistic treasures as well as adequate receptive structures and amusements for the seaside, religious, "green" and eno-gastronomic tourism.

SEASIDE RESORTS

Visiting this part of the Adriatic means enjoying the spectacle of two of the very few headlands on the entire coastline, San Bartolo and Ardizio, taking advantage of the tranquility of small isolated coves or experiencing the more frequented yet just as inviting sandy beaches.

Forty kilometers of soft sand stretching from Gabicce to Marotta, with an abundance of hotels, updated and reclassified over the years, and numerous campsites between Pesaro and Fano, where the beach is even wider and where the rocky shore creates safe havens for children, country houses and holiday farms for those who prefer to enjoy the sea while immersed in the green of the countryside.

To the north and Romagna lies the more popular resort of Gabicce Mare, where the splendors of the "Riviera" of the sixties still survives.

Pesaro, instead, located at the mouth of the river Foglia, with its approximately eight kilometers of fine sandy shore between the natural park of San Bartolo and Ardizio, offers a more relaxed lifestyle.

An ideal place for a family holiday or for those who prefer to take it easy far from the maddening crowd, though without renouncing the pleasures and fun that a holiday resort can offer. In summer, in fact, the entire area is alive with music, markets, food fairs, etc.

Further south, Fano has two beaches, the sandy Lido and the longer pebbled Sassonia that stretches as far as the mouth of the river Metauro.

Halfway along the Lido and Sassonia beaches lies Fano's picturesque fishing port, teeming with boats and the aroma of cooked fish (arrostite di pesce and brodetti alla marinara). Finally, at the southernmost end of the province and completing the "Pesaro and Urbino Riviera" stand the welcoming resorts of Torrette and Marotta.

Sports such as sailing, windsurfing and beach volley are possible along the entire coastline, which also has specially equipped play areas for children.

We can devote the afternoon to FANO.

FANO, a fine city, rich in monuments, about 12 km. (7 1/2) of coast road away, over the Canal Harbor. There is a fine Arch of Augustus; next it, the little church of San Michele with an elegant 16th century portal and the Loggias of San Michele. In the Piazza rises the 13th century Palazzo delta Ragione, of Lombard form, flanked by a Tower and the Palazzo Malatestiano (fine Gallery of Primitives). In the church of Santa Maria Nuova there is a Madonna and Saints and an Annunciation by Perugino. Leaving Fano the next day we reach (25 km. – 15 3/4 mi.) FOSSOMBRONE, a pretty town in the Metauro Valley with a 16th century Palazzo Comunale and many others, all with rhomboid rustication. Five kilometers farther on, turn right before entering the Furlo Gorge, to follow the Metauro (15 km. – 9 1/2 mi.) to URBINO.

Urbino

Urbino, a parallelogram lying over its two hills it keeps the form given it by its lord, Federico da Montefeltro. It was the birthplace of Bramante and Raphael. If he arrives from Faro, we advise the traveller to go in by the Via Nazionale, so as to get the southern aspect of the Ducal Palace, with its soaring turrets and storeys of loggias.

And so to the Palace, built by Luciano Laurana (1466), one of the most extraordinary examples of early Renaissance architecture, with its splendid Main Courtyard, the staircase which Vasari described as the finest of his time, the magnificent rooms with carved ceilings and inlaid mantelpieces.

On the first floor is the National Gallery of the Marches, an extremely rich collection, with two works by Piero della Francesca, Flagellation of Christ and a Madonna, Raphael's , Dumb Girl, and paintings by Verrocchio, Gentile da Fabriano, Giovanni Bellini, Paolo Uccello, Giovanni Sanzio (Raphael's father), Titian etc. Opposite the right wing of the Palace, the church of San Domenico, with a fine portal.

The city of Urbino (35 km from Pesaro) was the Duke's capital and is certainly the main attraction for any visitor to the Province of Pesaro and Urbino.

It is a city full of interest and surprise – the magnificent Ducal Palace (which houses the Galleria Nazionale delle Marche), the numerous art treasures to be found in its beautiful churches and monasteries, Raphael's birthplace and the many houses built by wealthy families which stand around the city's streets and alleys.

Around the city is that same panorama of hills and valleys that we see in the paintings of the great Renaissance masters who came to know and love Urbino during the time of the Montefeltro and Della Rovere dukes.

View from Urbino

Passing to Piazza della Repubblica and along Via Mazzini, one arrives at the Oratory of San Giovanni with excellent frescoes by the Salimbeni brothers. We now go back the Via Flaminia along the same road (14 km. – 8 /4 mi.) and pass through the Furlo Gorge to Acqualagna and CAGLI a town of severe appearance with a 15th century Palazzo Comunale and the Gothic-Romanesque church of San Francesco (frescoes inside), to rise through fine scenery to Scheggia at 55 km. (34 1/2 mi.) from Urbino.

Cagli

Here turn to the right and take the road which after 13 kms. (8 mi.) through bare, harsh mountain scenery, brings us into Umbria and to GUBBIO.

Gubbio

Gubbio - Palazzo dei Consoli

Gubbio is an ancient city which a perfectly preserved medieval atmosphere. Entering through Porto Metauro, we climb the Via dei Consoli, between ancient house-fronts, running past the austere Palazzo del Bargello to the impressive Piazza della Signoria, opening like a balcony supported on heavy arches, over the lower city and the plain beyond.

The piazza is dominated by the superb Palazzo dei Consoli (1332) opposite which rises the Palazzo Camomile of the same period (Picture Gallery inside).

Behind the palace rises Monte Ingino, towards which we climb up the steep Via Ducale to the Cathedral (13th cent.), with its austere interior sup ported on ten Gothic arches; with fine primitive paintings. Opposite is the Ducal Palace, by Laurana, with its beautiful courtyard. There is a magnificent view from up here.

Gubbio - Duomo interior

Returning to Piazza della Signoria we go down to the San Giovanni Battista district, with the church of San Giovanni, then on down Via Piccardi past sturdy medieval facades to the 14th century church of San Domenico, not far from the Roman Amphitheatre of the Augustan age.

Gubbio's townscape is dominated by the massive structure of the Palazzo dei Consoli, symbol of Gubbio's medieval power and one of the most beautiful public palaces in Italy.

Built between 1332 and 1337 and attributed by some critics to Gattapone and by others to Angelo da Orvieto, the building, elegant and majestic, has plain and simple walls decorated by a row of windows in its upper story; above there are a series of hanging arches and a Guelph battlement.

Notable is the fan shaped staircase leading, through a Gothic portal, to the large entrance hall, used in the Middle Ages for city assemblies. Now the Palazzo dei Consoli houses the Civic

Museum and the important Picture Gallery, containing works by local painters as well as by Tuscan masters.

Another building of great interest in Gubbio is the Palazzo Ducale: of very ancient Lombard origin and restructured at the end of the 15th century by order of Federico da Montefeltro, it is an important example of Renaissance architecture. The inner courtyard, built of stones and bricks, is splendid, and the interior is extremely elegant: unfortunately when the palace became a private property the furnishings were dispersed and today one may admire the Duke's studio – made of inlaid and carved wood – at the Metropolitan Museum of New York.

In front of this building stands the Cathedral, a Gothic 14th century church built where there was an older one; the facade, restored in the 16th century, has a beautiful Gothic portal and is decorated with the symbols that represent the Evangelists and the Mystic Lamb, the latter a testimony to the older structure. Its interior has a nave characterized by ten great Gothic arches that support the roof. This church contains interesting paintings and a splendid Flemish cope made of golden brocade.

In the Piazza 40 Martiri is situated the Church of S. Francesco, built in Gothic style in the 13th century and attributed, but not definitively, to Fra' Bevignate; the facade, uncompleted and altered, has a Gothic portal, a row of hanging arches and a small rose-window coming from the church of S. Francesco in Foligno. The interior has a nave with two aisles, and contains a rich painting decoration; the chapel in the right apse is dedicated to St. Francis and they say it was built above the Spadalongas' house, where the Saint took the habit.

In Gubbio there are many other buildings of historic and cultural interest: the Palazzo Pretorio, situated on the Piazza della Signoria opposite the Palazzo dei Consoli, built at the half of the 15th century by Gattapone in the Gothic style; the Palazzo del Bargello, very elegant medieval house; the Church of S. Maria della Vittoria, the so-called Vittorina: near a Franciscan monastery, it was one of the places frequented by St. Francis and, according tradition, it was here that took place the meeting between the Saint and the savage wolf, the famous wolf of Gubbio; the beautiful Gothic Church of S. Giovanni Battista; the Church of S. Domenico, with notable paintings; other small churches, noble palaces or simpler houses, the alleys, the wonderful landscape; and also the famous Fountain of the mad: they say that it's sufficient to run round it three times to be admitted in the category.

The Basilica of S. Ubaldo: the church, dedicated to St. Ubaldo, bishop and patron Saint of the town of Gubbio, has a medieval origin, but was enlarged in 1514 by order of the Duchesses Elisabetta and Eleonora Della Rovere. It has a fine 16th century portal and a delightful Franciscan cloister. Its interior is divided into five aisles and on the major altar is placed the Renaissance urn that preserves the relics of St. Ubaldo, brought here in 1194. In the aisle on the left are housed the Candles.

The Basilica may be reached either by road or by a cable-car: departure from the center of Gubbio, near Porta Romana, and in few minutes' trip one arrives at the Basilica, on the slope of the

Mount Ingino, enjoying a magnificent panoramic view of the town and the valley below.

Along other streets of the higher city (Via Savelli, with fine palaces) one can get to Santa Maria Nacre, with fine frescoes by Ottaviano Nelli. Then down to the tower of Porta Romana, beyond which stands Sant'Agostino, an impressive 13th century building with beautiful primitive frescoes in the interior and out of Gribbin on to a fine panoramic road through the hills leading to PERUGIA.

Corsa dei Ceri (Gubbio, May)

The Corsa dei Ceri is one of the most spectacular fascinating folk events in Umbria: the three teams devoted to St. Antonio, St. Giorgio, St. Ubaldo (Gubbio's saint patron) have to run among jamming crowds, spurred on by their shouts and cheers, whilst carrying high wooden columns on top of which the saint statue is held, until they reach the church of Saint Ubaldo.

Perugia

Perugia Palazzo dei Priori

Perugia is the capital city in the region of Umbria in central Italy, near the Tiber river, and the capital of the province of Perugia.

Perugia is an important artistic center of Italy. The town gave his nickname to the famous painter Pietro Vannucci, called Perugino, who worked in Perugia, Rome and Florence. Perugino is said to be the *Maestro* of Raffaello, who left in Perugia five paintings (today no longer in the city) and one fresco. Another famous painter, Pinturicchio, lived in Perugia. In Galeazzo Alessi Perugia found its most famous architect.

Visiting Perugia in one day

PERUGIA, This important Etruscan city, built on a hill overlooking the Tiber valley, became a Roman municipality; and the Middle Ages and the Renaissance have given it the severe and noble aspect it bears today. The artistic center of the city is the Piazza IV Novembre, in the middle of which stands the Fontana Maggiore (1275), decorated by Nicolo and Giovanni Pisano.

On one side of the square stretches the massive wall of the Gothic Cathedral (inside, sculptures and paintings and a Madonna by Luca Signorelli in the Museum), and on the opposite side, the bold Palazzo dei Priori (built in the 13th century, but enlarged over the next two centuries) from whose severe facade jut the bronze statues of the Griffon and the Lion, emblems of the city.

The exquisite main Door of the Palace opens on to the nearby Corso Vannueci; on the second floor is the National Gallery of Umbria, a magnificent collection of paintings in 25 rooms, with Umbrian primitives works by Duccio di Buoninsegna, Gentile da Fabriano, Begin Angelica, Piero della Francesca, Benozzo Gozzoli, Pinturicchio, and Perugino, as well as outstanding medieval and Renaissance sculptures.

Next door, in the same street, is Collegio del Cambia, seat of the money-changers of old, whose lavish Audience Chamber contains excellent frescoes by Perugino, set in precious carved wooden frames. Leaving the building, we take Via dei Priori, in a rough medieval setting and passing the church of S, Filippo Neri, with its Baroque facade, we descend through a network of narrow old streets, to an extremely picturesque spot, where the tall Tower of the Sciri (12th century), the Mardorla Gate, dating from Etruscan times, and the exquisitely pure Renaissance facade of the Madonna della Luce (1518) are grouped together.

From here, we come to the spacious piazza San Francesco where, standing side by side we see the gentle facade of the

Oratorio di San Bernardino, with delicate hasrelief by Agostino di Duccio (1461), and the Gothic church of S. Francesco (1230).

Fontana Maggiore

We suggest returning to Via dei Priori, and them taking, still behind the Palace, the extremely ancient Via della Gabbia, so as to get to the impressive bend in the street, called Maesta delle Volte, one of the most awesome medieval spots in Italy.

We walk down to Piazza Morlacchi and, by way of Via Cesare Battisti, come to the so-called Arch of Augustus, a superb Etruscan gate, with a 16th century loggin at the top of the left-hand bastion. In Piazza Fortebraccio stands Palazzo Gallenga (18th century), which today accommodates the University for Foreigners.

Taking Corso Garibaldi, we reach the Church of S. Angelo (5th-6th century), the oldest in Perugia (but elegant in its unassuming simplicity. Returning along Corso Garibaldi, we reach the beautiful Gothic church of S. Agostino (inside, magnificent wooden Choirstalls by B. D'Agnolo, 1502, and an excellent painting by Guercino). Returning to Piazza Fortebraccio, we go up Via Pinturicchio to the extremely ancient chapel of S. Severo with a fresco by Raphael, the only work by him in Perugia. Nearby is the so-called Sun Gate (Porta del Sole – perhaps from the name of an ancient temple, dedicated to the Sun), from which we head towards the solitary Piazza Michelotti, the highest point in the city, with a magnificent view of the surrounding plain and the mountains and Assisi.

Taking Via della Viola and Via Alessi, we come to Piazza Matteotti where, beyond the Church of the Gesu (1572), we see the Lombard Palazzo del Capitano del Popolo (1481), and the long Palazzo della Vecchia Universita 1483). Passing by the facade of S. Maria del Popolo and turning up towards the busy Corso Vannucci, we finish off our morning tour in one of the restaurants in the center of town.

Perugia by night

From Corso Vannucci we will return to Piazza Matteotti and take Via Oberdan where, making our way down among interesting buildings, we come to the towering octagonal Gothich church of S. Ercolano, fromwhich we reach the Etruscan Marcia Gate. Taking Via Marzia, we enter the subterranean Via Bagliona, where once stood the old houses of the Baglioni family, the lords of Perugia; in 1540, commissioned by Paul III, Antonio da Sangallo used them as the foundation for his Rocca Paolina, which was unfortunately destroyed in the uprisings of 1848.

We now enter Corso Cavour which takes us to San Domenico, a Gothic church with a handsome interior illuminated by a magnificent Stained-glass Window (the striking Gothic tomb of Pope Benedict XI, wooden Chairstalls, sculptures, by Agostino di Duccio). Next to the church, m a former convent, is the Archaeological and Prehistoric Museum, richly endowed with Etruscan and Roman bronzes and sculptures. Continuing down Corso Cavour, we pass by the stupendous Porm San Pietro (1475) by A. di Duccio and come to the Church of San Pietro (originally 10th century, but transformed) with a 15th century bell-tower and an outstanding, extremely rich interior, decorated with extraordinary works of art, including a Piela by Perugino and what are perhaps the most beautiful wooden Choir-stalls (1526) in Italy. Retracing our steps to Viale Roma, we can climb up to S.Giuliana, a Romanesque church with a most beautiful 14th century Gothic cloister. We then return into the city, our visit of what at least are its essential aspects having come to an end.

Assisi

Assisi view

On the morning of the next day, we leave Perugia by Via Roma and after a drive of 15 miles come to ASSISI.

Assisi is a town in Italy in Perugia province, Italy, in the Umbria region, on the western flank of Mt. Subasio. It is the birthplace of St. Francis, who founded the Franciscan religious order in the town in 1208, and St. Clare (Chiara d'Offreducci), the founder of the Poor Clares. Saint Gabriel of Our Lady of Sorrows of the 19th century was also born in Assisi.

Half day visit to Assisi

ASSISI, an ancient and noble city perched on a spur of Mt. Subasio. We enter by St. Peter's Gate and go straight to the imposing group of buildings consisting of the church and convent of San Francesco, which loom high over the valley. As soon as St. Francis died (1226), work was started on the building of this vast two-storey basilica which when it was finished, at the end of the 13th century, all the finest painters of the period were called to decorate.

Thus was born one of the most extensive series of fresco-cycles in the history of painting. From Cimabue to the unknown Maestro di S. Francesco, from Pietro Lorenzetti to Simone Martini, from Giotto to his pupil, Maso, known as Giottino throngs of unknown disciples, all the painters of that time in Central Italy worked in these two superimposed churches.

A visit must also be made to the Cloister in order to admire the marvelous Apse, of rare and virile strength.

Assisi square

Taking Via San Francesco, we then go to the Piazza del Comune, dominated above by the medieval Castle, where Frederick II of Swabia lived for much of his boyhood. The post important building in the square is the Roman Temple of Minerva, almost perfectly preserved, the interior having subsequently been converted into a church. Beneath the square are the remains of the Roman Forum. After a short walk we come to San Rufino, the cathedral of Assisi, with its lofty 12th century Romanesque façade.

From here we go down to the church of Santa Chiara, with ifs great rose-window and its delicate white and pink stone exterior (1265); along the side, 14th century buttresses built with a view, to guaranteeing stability of the building. Inside we may see frescoes and panel-paintings by primitive artists. We then pass on to the Romanesque church of San Pietro (13th century), with its three great rosewindows, and from here, through the picturesque medieval streets, back to San Francesco

Spello

After the visit to Assisi, we leave, descending into the valley and passing by the enormous church of S. Maria degli Angeli, and go toward Perugia, but without re-entering the city. When we come to Ponte San Giovanni (12 1/2 miles from Assisi), we take Highway No. 3 his to the right, up the valley of the Tiber, and after some 20 miles come to UMBERTIDE, with its Castle (14th century) and the beautiful octagonal church of S. Maria della Reggia (16th century). In the church of S. Croce (1651), we find a Deposition by Luca Signorelli.

Spello

Thirteen kilometers from Assisi (8 mi.) lies Spello, on the last spur of Monte Subiaso. We enter the town through the fine Roman Porta Consolare and climb up past ancient house-fronts to the Oratory of San Bernardino (Madonna by Pinturicchio) and Santa Maria Maggiore with its fine frescoes by Pinturicchio and paintings of his school.

Passing Sant'Andrea (13th cent.) with more paintings by Pinturicchio and the Palazzo Comunale we climb to the Belvedere near the walls of the ancient fortress and the ruins of a Roman Arch. The view from here is superb, looking over the Umbrian hills to Perugia and Assisi.

Spello (in Antiquity: Hispellum) is an ancient town and commune (township) of Italy, in the province of Perugia in east central Umbria, on the lower southern flank of Mt. Subasio. It is 6 km (4 mi) NNW of Foligno and 10 km (6 mi) SSE of Assisi.

The old walled town lies on a regularly NW-SE sloping ridge that eventually meets the plain.

Spello - window

From the top of the ridge, Spello commands a good view of the Umbrian plain towards Perugia; at the bottom of the ridge, the town spills out of its walls into a small modern section (or Borgo) served by the rail line from Rome to Florence via Perugia.

Populated in ancient times by the Umbri, it became a Roman colony in the 1st century BC. Under the reign of Constantine the Great it was called Flavia Constans, as attested by a document preserved in the local Communal Palace.

The densely-inhabited town, built of stone, is of decidedly medieval aspect, and is enclosed in a circuit of medieval walls on Roman foundations, including three Roman Late Antique gates (Porta Consolare, Porta di Venere and the "Arch of Augustus") and traces of three more, remains of an amphitheater, as well several medieval gates. Spello boasts about two dozen small churches, most of them medieval.

S. Maria Maggiore

Santa Maria Maggiore

Santa Maria Maggiore (known from 1159), probably built over an ancient temple dedicated to Juno and Vesta.

The facade has a Romanesque portal and a 13th century bell tower, while the pilasters next to the apse have frescoes by Perugino (1512). The most striking feature is however a very fine chapel (Cappella Bella) frescoed by Pinturicchio.

The Umbrian artist was called to paint it in 1500 by Troilo Baglioni, after he had just finished the Borgia Apartment's decoration. The cycle include the Annunciation, the Nativity and the Dispute with the Doctors, plus four Sibyls in the vault. The Palazzo dei Canonici, annexed to the church, houses the Town's Art Gallery.

Foligno

Going back to the State Highway, another few miles brings us to FOLIGNO, which we enter by crossing the picturesque Canale dei Molini (Mill-race) and coming out into Piazza Centrale on one corner of this stands Palazzo Trinci, containing a fine chapel frescoed by Nelli, a Museum and an Art Gallery.

Foligno - Piazza San Domenico

The Palazzo Comunale has a Neo-Classical facade and a 15th century tower. To be seen then the Palazzo Orfini of the 15 century and the graceful sidewall wail of the Romanesque Cathedral, with rose-windows mothered windows and a fine 13th century Portal.

After Foligno, we leave the State Highway for a side road leading to the enchanting town of MONTEFALCO.

Montefalco

Montefalco

MONTEFALCO, (12 km – 7 1/2 mi.). It is in a superb position, girt by massive battlemented walls. In its churches of Santa Chiara, Sant'Agostino, Madonna del Soccorso, San Fortunato but especially of San Francesco, three generations of Umbrian painters in the 14th and 15th centuries left an unbelievable complex of frescoes, quite exceptional for a little place of only 7000 inhabitants. A call here is made essential if only for the beautiful work of Benozzo Gozzoli. The road brings us back to the State Highway after winding for 23 km. (14 1/2 mi.) near TREVI perched on its hill. Two kilometers (1 1/4 mi.) farther on is the little Roman Temple beside the Fonti di Clitunno (springs) in a charming woodland setting. Another 16 km. (10 mi.) brings us to Spoleto where we advise the visitor who is not in a hurry to go first to the cemetery see the extremely rare Basilica of San Salvatore with intact facade and apse of the 4th century and a severe Roman interior. Going back on to the Via Nursina and crossing the bridge, we now enter SPOLETO.

Spoleto

Spoleto

Spoleto was a proud Etruscan city, then Roman; it became the seat of a powerful Longobard Duchy in the early Middle Ages. In Piazza Garibaldi is the 12th century church of San Gregorio Magno, and near it, a Roman bridge. Going along Via Anfiteatro, skirting the ruins of the Roman Amphitheatre which Totila. transformed into a fortress in 545, we go up Via Cecili as far as Porto Fuga (12th century) near Palazzo Cecili (15th century) and on up to Piazza Torre dell'Olio, near the massive city wall with superimposed Etruscan, Roman,Longobard, medieval and Renaissance work. We continue to climb past ancient buildings, all vaults and towers, to Piazza San Domenico, with its 14th century church, in bands of white and red stone.

From here it is only a few steps to the piazza in which Palazzo Collicola stands. In this area there is the little Romanesque church of San Lorenzo. Here one takes Via delle Terme for the ruins of the Roman Theatre in Palazzo Ancaiani.

Starting from Piazza della Liberta one can get to the small church of Sant'Ansano, beside which stands the Arch of Drusus (23 AD) leading into Piazza del Mercato, the center of the medieval city. Turning left off this we enter Piazza della Genga with Palazzo della Genga and the Fontana Grande, or Great Fountain. Piazza Municipio, reached along Via dei Duchy, contains the 13th century Municipal Hall m which there is an Art Gallery. Passing from the panoramic Piazza Campello and Via Saffi into Via dell'Arringo, we go down the wide steps leading to the superb Cathedral, inside which there is sculpture by Bernini,frescoes by Lippo Lippi and the latter's tomb.

From Spoleto to TERNI is 26 km. of mountain road (16 3/4 mi.).

Terni

Marmore waterfalls

TERNI. As one enters, it is best to make for Piazza Tacito and then along Via Fratti to the 13th century church of San Francesco, inside which there are 14th century frescoes inspired by Dante's Divine Comedy. Going along Via Nobili and Via Fratini and then Via Cavour brings us to the Cathedral, with a 17th century facade ascribed to Bernini, whose loggia opens into the Romanesque Portal.

There is a fine 10th century crypt. Opposite the Cathedral the fine Palazzo Bianchini-Riccardi by Antonio da Sangallo the Younger and, to the right, the rums of the Roman Amphitheatre. Via Vescovado, Via Roma and then Via del Popolo take us to the city's finest church, San Salvatore, whose 12th century nave was built onto an ancient Temple of the Sun Passing the majestic Palazzo Spada brings us to Piazza del Popolo and so we leave Term by Ponte Garibaldi along a fine road which takes us past the Marmore Cascades (8 km. – 5 mi.) and Lake Piediluco and minor lakes to RIETI.

Rieti

Rieti

Immediately on entering the town of Rieti after Piazza Marconi is San Domenico (13th century) on the right. From here to Piazza Battisti with the Cathedral; Romanesque with Renaissance facade ad fine campanile; and the Bishop's Palace. Close at hand, the picturesque Vescovado Vaults (1288). Via Roma has fine Gothic houses and leads to San Pietro Apostolo with a 13th century Romanesque portal: close by is the late Renaissance Palazzo Vecchiarelli Ponte Romano crosses the River Velino, on to which picturesque houses front. To the left here stands San Francesco (1285) with a Gothic Altar and frescoes. In the Baroque Palazzo del Municipio the Civic Museum is housed, with some good works such as paintings by Antoniazzo Romano and his pupils, Luca di Tome, archaeological exhibits and a fine 15th century German Pieta. Leaving the town by Porta d'Arci, note the massive Walls (13th century) which still surround the town.

L'Aquila

One leaves Rieti by State Highway No. 4, commanded to the left by Monte Terminillo. After Cittaducale, perched high on a hill, one posses wooded valleys to arrive at ANTRODOCO (25 km. – 16 mi. from Rieti). This is an ancient town at the foot of Monte Giano. Here we leave the River Velino and go up a majestic valley, through road tunnels and narrow gorges to arrive at Sella di Caron. Here we are at 3212 ft and the setting is Alp ne. From here we go down into the bowl of the hills in which L'AOUILA lies.

Downtown L'Aquila before the earthquake

L'Aquila: its monuments are scattered at random round the outskirts. Beginning from the modern Piazza del Duomo, go up to Santa Maria di Paganica, a fine Romanesque church of 1308, surrounded by noteworthy 15th century palaces. From here we can go on to the superb Castle built in 1535 by the Spanish Viceroy, who had been frightened by a revolt of the Aquilans in 1529. Magnificent view over the city and the mountains, among which the Gran Sasso d'Italia stands out.

From the Castle, down to San Bernardino, a fine 15th century Basilica built over the tomb of the Sienese saint who died here in 1444: inside, carved ceilings, fine Renaissance sculpture.

Going down the majestic monumental staircase in front of the church into the picturesque Via Fortebraccio and turning to the right before reaching Porta di Bazzano, we enter the old quarter, where the severe Romanesque facade of Santa Giusta rises.

Fountain of the 99 Jets

Then back to Porta di Bazzano, go through it and climb up to Santa Maria di Collemaggio, one of the most beautiful churches in Italy, whose majestic facade is relieved by three portals, three rose-windows and inlaid work of tiny red and white stones (13th century). Going back to Porta Bazzano, go towards Corso Federico II and beyond it to San Marco, with a fine Romanesque portal. Via Arcivescovado has several fine palaces: in Via San Marciano, which is near, there is the House of Nardis, with Gothic arches and the church of San Marciano from which one may proceed to Santa Maria di Roio (15th cent.) surrounded by noteworthy palaces. Via Fontesecca takes us down to the famous Fountain of the 99 Jets, near which stands the splendid Romanesque church of San Vito.

Returning to the city, one may visit San Domenico, San Pietro in Coppito and the 14th century San Silvestro.

L'Aquila after the earthquake

In the Castle there is an important National Museum of the Abruzzo (sculpture, paintings and objets d'art). The seventh day of the journey begins with the ascent to Assergi (21 km. – 13 mi.)with a fine Romanesque church of 1150, lower station of the bold cableway of 3400 meters to Campo Imperatore (2114 meters – 6934 ft.). All around, the peaks of the Gran Sasso and a vast panorama of the Abruzzo mountains and plains. On the eighth day we leave L'Aquila by Porta Napoli. After 8 km. (5 mi.) we come to Bazzano, with its beautiful rustic Romanesque church of Santa Giusta. From here we climb to Poggio Picenze, leaving the Barisciano turning. It would be worth the trouble, however, to make a short deviation (5 km. – 3 mi.) for BOMINACO for its splendid Romanesque churches of San Pellegrino and Santa Maria. Back on the State ighway take the straight over the Navelli plateau-beautiful country-and then down into the River Pescara valley to POPOLI at the foot of the mountains (50 km. – 28 1/4 mi.) from L'Aquila. Here there is the fine 15th century church of San Francisco and the Gothic Ducat Tavern.

Popoli

Popoli

From Popoli, passing the CORFINIO turning after 5 km (3 mi.) we reach SULMONA, an ancient city with fine buildings. The 13th century Cathedral is on the left as you enter; Palazzo dell'Annunziata, the finest civic building in the Abruzzi, a synthesis of styles trouble, however, to make a short deviation (5 km. – 3 mi.) for BOMINACO for its splendid Romanesque churches of San Pellegrino and Santa Maria. Back on the State Highway take the straight over the Navelli plateau-beautiful country-and then down into the River Pescara valley to POPOLI at the foot of the mountains (50 km. – 28 3/4 mi.) from L'Aquila. Here there is the fine 15th century church of San Francesco and the Gothic Ducal Tavern.

From Popoli we suggest making a deviation of 14 km. (8 3/4 mi.) to TORRE DE' PASSERI to see the architectural masterpiece of the Abruzzi, the Romanesque Abbey of San Clemente at Casauria, a splendid monumental complex built between the 9th and the 12th centuries; it is to be seen both for its architectural splendor and for its carvings.

Rivisondoli - Roccaraso

Rivisondoli

From Popoli, passing the CORFINIO turning after 5 km (3 mi.) we reach SULMONA, an ancient city with fine buildings. The 13th century Cathedral is on the left as you enter; Palazzo dell'Annunziata, the finest civic building in the Abruzzi, a synthesis of styles running from Gothic to Baroque: in the interior, Civic Museum with a statue of Ovid, who was born here: the Romanesque church of San Francesco alla Scarpa. In the airy Piazza del Mercato, we see the arches of a 14th century acqueduct which feeds the 16th century fountain, Fontana del Vecchio ; at the foot of the mountain stands San Filippo. Leaving the XIV century rustic Porta Napoli we climb to century RIVISONDOLI (1210 m. – 3969 ft.) a mountain resort, where we shall spend the night, or in nearby ROCCARASO.

Chieti

Chieti

The next day we set out on the beautiful "ring road of the Abruzzi", a long balcony commanding most stupendous views . It runs along the massif of the Maiella 2800 m. – 9164 ft.) towards Lama dei Peligni (2298 ft.) and GUARDIAGRELE at 61 km. 37 3/4 mi.) from Rivisondoli, bring us to CHIETI.

CHIETI, ancient Teate standing on a pleasant hill with fine views over the Maiella, the Gran Sasso and the Adriatic.

Outstanding monuments to visit: the Roman ruins of the city include three small temples of the late I century AD, the Roman theatre, the barbs of the I century AD with a large storage tank dug into the hillside.

The cathedral with a slender bell tower of the 15th century and a rich Baroque crypt containing the silver bust of St Justin by Nicola da Guardiagrele. The Archaeological Museum rich in finds ranging from the VII century BC to the II century AD, including the famous statue of the "Warrior of Capestrano" of the late VI century BC and the well-stocked provincial library with precious incunabula and the Mss of "Il Piacere" and "La Figlia di Jorio" by Gabriele d'Annunzio.

Pescara

Pescara

Leaving Chieti drive towards the Adriatic, reaching, after 12 miles PESCARA, the largest and most up-to-date city in Abruzzo, birthplace of Gabriele d'Annunzio. Worthy of a visit are: d'Annunzio's birthplace, the stela of the d'Annunzio Memorial Theatre and the painting, by F.P. Michetti, of "The Daughter of Jorio" in the Palazzo della Provincia.

PESCARA has 6 1/2 miles of seaside promenade, wide sandy beaches and a large number of bathing stations; it has become the most popular resort in the Mid-Adriatic. On the tenth day take the splendid seaside drive that links Francavilla through the Pescara pinewood to the important resort of MONTESILVANO, from which leave the coast to climb along the national highway up the eastern slopes of the Gran Sasso to LORETO APRUTINO, a pretty town on a hill; there are 12th-13th century frescoes in the church of Santa Maria in Piano (13th cent.).

The Acerbo Gallery contains ancient Abruzzo pottery.

Teramo

From here it is a short distance to PENNE (19 mi. from Pescara), a city of proud Roman, medieval and Risorgimento traditions. To be seen: the church of San Domenico and that of the Annunziata, the Cathedral, the church of Santa Maria in Colleromano; another 26 kms (16 1/4 mi.) brings us to the turning for ATRI with a splendid Romanesque Cathedral (Gothic interior with fine frescoes-the most important cycle in the Abruzzi) and other Romanesque churches. From Atri the road descends to the sea again (15 km. – 9 1/2 mi.) at Pineto degli Abruzzi, from which one arrives at GIULIANOVA. There may be time for a swim at Giulianova before climbing up again to TERAMO

Teramo

TERAMO (25 km. – 15 1/2 mi.) an ancient Picenian city which later became Roman and then Longobard. Fine Cathedral with richly decorated Portal (1332), in which there is the frontal by Nicola da Guardiagrele and a superb Altar-Piece by Iacobello del Fiore (15th century).

On the next day of the journey we leave Teramo early in the morning for 37 km. (23 mi.) of driving through mountains and gorges which bring us to ASCOLI PICENO.

Ascoli Piceno

Ascoli Piceno

Ascoli Piceno, an inhabited center since the Bronze Age, rich in Romanesque and medieval monuments. This wonderful city will come as a complete surprise to the foreign visitor, who may very well never have heard of it. Our program envisages seeing it on the afternoon of the eleventh day and the morning of the twelfth. We will begin at Piazza del Popolo, which for its sober elegance is one of the finest piazzas in Italy.

On one side is the massive Palazzo del Popolo (13th cent.) with its Renaissance portal (inside there is an Archaeological Museum).

Through a perspective of two small battlemented 16th century palaces, we see at one end the side wall, apses and slim hexagonal bell-towers of San Francesco. Near the porch of this church, in Corso Mazzini, is the elegant Merchants' Loggia (15th century) which continues the architecture of the facade, one side is open and is used as a busy market, the other is closed, silent and peaceful.

In Piazza dell'Arringo rises the magnificent 17th century Palazzo dell'Arringo or del Comune with tall caryatids flanking the windows (inside a rich Art Gallery with works by, primitives, Carlo Crivelli, Titian, Correggio, Magnasco, Reni, Rubens, Canaletto).

Opposite are the Cathedral and the superb Romanesque Baptistery, built over a Roman temple. In Via Bonaparte stands the fine Palazzo Bonaparte 16th century Lombard work. Taking Vial, Repubblica past the Public Gardens we reach San Vittore, a pretty Romanesque church; along Corso Mazzini we arrive at Palazzo Malaspina, an imaginatively built and rather rough building of the 16th century, with a loggia supported on columns carved to look like tree-trunks.

Going right, along Via Sacconi we arrive at the River Trento by the ancient solitary Porta Tufilla through which, proceeding along Via Bartolomei, we arrive at Santa Maria Inter Vineas: here at hand there are the churches of San Vincenzo with its very rare Romanesque coffered facade and a Romanesque portal, and San Pietro Martire. Go as far as the Roman Bridge and then turn back along Via Soderini with its fine Lombard House, wander through the streets of the fine medieval quarter with its towers, the ancient severity of its house-fronts and the Romanesque church of San Giacomo, the Roman Porta Gemina, the Gothic church of Sant'Agostino, opposite which are the two Towers which give the street its name – Via delle Torri.

Leave Ascoli by Porta Romana and turn left off the Via Salaria after 8 km. (5 mi.) to climb between steep mountain slopes (to the left Monte Vettore 2422 m. – 7933 ft.) to Comunanza (34 km. – 21 1/4 mi.) and 9 km. (5314 mi.) farther on AMANDOLA with the fine 15th century churches of Sant'Agostino and San Franceseo (frescoes).

The road then drops to SARNANO, a fine medieval town with the churches of Santa Maria di Piazza and San Franceseo (inside a rare panel painting by Crivelli) and so to URBISAGLIA perched on a hill, with its massive 14th century Castle to reach finally at 49 km. (30 3/4 mi.) from Ascoli, the ABBEY OF FIASTRA (1141) a wonderful Romanesque Cistercian Basilica.

Fiastra Abbey Cloister

The church is dedicated to Santa Maria di Chiaravalle di Fiastra. Its architecture is in Romanesque-Burgundian style, and characterized by simplicity and austerity. Building materials for its construction were taken from the nearby Roman settlement of Urbs Salvia.

The most important elements of the abbey are arranged around the cloister, that is the heart of the monastery: here the monks would contemplate and meditate while walking, or sit under the arcade and study the Sacred Scriptures. A monumental well still stands in the middle and is connected to a cistern which receives rain-water.

Another 10 km. (6 1/4 mi.) brings us to MACERATA.

Macerata

Macerata

MACERATA, an ancient city in a pleasant hill setting between the Potenza and Chienti valleys. Its most curious monument is an old sports ground, the Neo-Classical Sferisferio (1829) built for the game of "pallone" once very popular in the Marches, and where opera seasons with famous international singers are new held every summer.

From here to the Baroque Cathedral (good tryptych by Nuzi in interior) near which we find the 18th century Madonna della Misericordia.

Along Via Don Minzoni, leaving Palazzo Marefossi to the right and the ancient University (1290) to the left, we reach Piazza Liberia with the Palazzo della Prefettura and the Merchants' Loggia (1490) and the Torre di Piazza.

There are fine buildings in Corso Matteotti including the 16th century Palazzo Ferri with rhomboid rustication. In the Art Gallery (Piazza Vittorio Veneto), fine primitive paintings and an expressive Madonna by Crivelli.

The next morning we go down into the valley of the Potenza to Villa Potenza (6 km. – 3 3/4 mi.) near which are the vast ruins of the Roman Helvia Retina, destroyed by the Visigoths.

Recanati Piazza Giacomo Leopardi

Turning to the right, one goes down into the valley, as far as RECANATI, birthplace of the great 19th century poet Giacomo Leopardi: there is a group of noteworthy churches here, including San Domenico, with frescoes by Lorenzo Lotto, Santa Maria di Montemorello next to be noted for a group of works by Lotto, paintings by primitives, Guercino etc.

Going farther down the valley (11 km. – Tam.) brings us to LORETO.

Loreto

Loreto - Piazza della Madonna

LORETO, a little town dominated by its Sanctuary, built by Sangallo, Andrea Sansovino and other architects (1518-1522) and containing an enormous wealth of works of art, in the church, the treasury and the adjoining Museum-marbles and bronzes by Benedetto da Maiano, Bandinelli, Sansovino etc., frescoes and panel and canvas paintings by Melozzo da Forli, Signorelli, Pomarancio, Garofalo, Lotto, Maratta, Rein, Domenichino, Caracci, Magnasco-and majolica work, tapestries and jewellery. After 4 km. (2 1/2 mi.) we reach PORTO RECANATI on the Adriatic and take the coast road which skirts the magnificent spur of Monte Conero, to Sirolo and its beautiful Romanesque church of Santa Maria di Portonovo by the sea. After 35 km. (21 1/2 mi.) we reach ANCONA.

Ancona

Ancona

ANCONA, a city with numerous monuments from all the periods in its long history. Entering by the Baroque Porta Pia at the southern extremity of the port we go towards Piazza Garibaldi. Within easy reach of this point we find the wonderful Portal of Sant'Agostino (1475) built on to a house when the church was demolished, the central Piazza della bepubblica with its Neo-classical Theatre, the Palazzo della Prefettura with its graceful courtyard, the ancient and curious "Fountain of the 33 Jets" and many rugged arches and severe medieval house-fronts. Wide steps lead us to the Baroque San Domenico to see Titian's Crucifixion and Guercino's Annunciation. Then we go to the Romanesque Church of San Pietro, with important sculpture and the Piazza del Senato and the very fine Palazzo del Senato which houses the National Museum of the Marches, one of the most important archaeological collections in Italy, particularly as regards pre-Roman Adriatic cultures.

Near here, in a fine palace overlooking the sea, is the important Art Gallery with works by Primitives and also by Crivelli, Lotto, an exceptional canvas by Titian etc. Opposite this palace the theatrical Church of the Gesu by Vanvitelli. It is best to ask the way to the Romanesque Santa Maria della Piazza, the most beautiful church in Ancona, with its facade composed of a striking series of superimposed Romanesque loggias. Close at hand is the Gothic Merchants' Loggia with noteworthy Renaissance sculpture. Then one must go the whole length of Via Vanvitelli to the Cathedral of San Ciriaco; there is no other cathedral in Italy which boasts such a position, overlooking a precipice into the sea on a lonely promontory. It is of Greek Cross plan with a marvelous porch resting on two carved lions. Lastly, on the end of the jetty there is a Roman Arch built in honor of Trajan, who built the port of Ancona.

On the last day of our journey we leave Ancona and turn off at 11 km. (7 mi.) to visit the ABBEY OF CHIARAVALLE (1172) 5 km. (3 mi.) inland. After another 12 km. (7 1/2 mi.) comes IESI where Frederick II of Swabia was born, with its beautiful Palazzo della Signoria (15th century) and a good Art Gallery.

Back on the coast road, we reach SENIGALLIA with its Cathedral, its 15th century Palazzo Comunale and the 17th century church della Croce, Three km. (1 3/4 mi.) farther on is the church of Santa Maria delle Grazie with a Renaissance cloister and a Perugino Madonna.

Then we take the coast road again, which in 34 km. along the coast (21 1/4 mi.) brings us back to Pesaro.

The Author

Enrico Massetti was born in Milano, Italy. Now he lives in Washington DC, USA, but he regularly visit his hometown, and enjoys going around all the places near his home town that can be reached by public transportation.

Enrico can be reached at enricomassetti@msn.com.

Other tourist e-guides

All tourist guides from Enrico Massetti are listed at http://enricomassetti.com/tourist-e-guides/ and can be purchased in printed form as well as in all digital formats at all major online stores.

These guides include:

Apulia

Bolzano - Bozen

Calabria

Cinque Terre

Ferrara

Florence and Tuscany

Florence in Two Days

Lake Como

Lake Garda

Lake Maggiore

Mantua a Complete Guide

Naples, Capri, Ischia and Pompeii

One Day in Bergamo Alta From Milan

Pisa in One Day

Portofino and the Riviera

Rome a Complete Guide

Sardinia

Sicily

The Great Dolomite Road Bolzano to Cortina

Turin

Umbria

Venice in Two, Three or More Days

Verona in One Day

Table of Contents

Central Italy: The Marches and Abruzzo 1
From Pesaro to Roccaraso 3
Pesaro 4
Urbino 7
Gubbio 10
    Corsa dei Ceri (Gubbio, May) 14
Perugia 15
    Visiting Perugia in one day 16
Assisi 20
Spello 22
Foligno 25
Montefalco 26
Spoleto 27
Terni 29
Rieti 30
L'Aquila 31
Popoli 34
Rivisondoli - Roccaraso 35
Chieti 36
Pescara 37
Teramo 38
Ascoli Piceno 39
Macerata 42
Loreto 44
Ancona 45

The Author	47
Other tourist e-guides	48

Printed in Great Britain
by Amazon